NO WORRIES!

COPYRIGHT

1. INTRODUCTION

A friend said to me "Ian you never *seem* to worry about anything" I replied "Jon, you are not totally correct I *do not* worry about anything" and I really do not. I cannot predict my future. I cannot change my past. I do know exactly, where I am at this moment in time. Ten years ago, I worried about everything and I now know why. Everything I did revolved around taking chances and every time I took another chance, I became deeper and deeper into every type of debt. This lifestyle was putting my health and lifetime at risk. I began to realise Happiness was the positive emotion I needed to introduce into my lifetime. Worry was the negative emotion I had to escape from. I began to work toward this goal.

I began to write about my lifetime. I left nothing out, as I wrote the words, I totally accepted what a fool I had become. I thought very deeply about the mistakes and failures of my life, and at some point I realised it was time to move on. I have never looked back and I never will.

My desire, is that you will come to the *sane* conclusion, there really is no point in letting anything worry you. I accepted my beliefs had become my real enemies. Where did the seeds of my beliefs come from? Poor parental guidance? Poor choice of friends? Poor educational decisions? I have no idea. I did realise, I could not think properly, my mind was full of false expectations which I believed could become realities. I could sense my potentials, and many times I tasted the unripened fruit of those potentials. Unfortunately I did not understand how to make my potentials become fixed realities.

Many times I saw the flickering flame of success extinguished and I was left in the darkness of failure once again, my craving for success made me cut corners, even the greatest of my ideas were doomed to failure due to impatience and not accepting the importance of learning the how? And the why? You may learn the how (education) and the why (freedom) as you read the book.

I firmly believe that those who live in reality are more able to feel a real happiness. We can never be totally happy when we are not free to do as one pleases. After a day, week, month, year or even a decade of worthy effort, all of us must be rewarded in some way, for the effort we put into our lives. We should always have an objective to fulfil, even if the objective is years ahead (for example paying off a mortgage) the objective fuels the effort.

The ways in which we think and reason with ideas, are two of the keys to success and happiness. One of the ways we can gauge success is from the amount of personal freedom we can access during our lifetimes. Your body is your most valuable possession, your mind your most powerful asset, time is your most valuable commodity. Your body, mind and the lifetime you enjoy are given to you, you did not choose to be here, you are here because of a chance encounter in the evolution of the universe. Your body, thoughts and encounters become your "being". Make certain you gain enough freedom to enjoy *being* in your lifetime.

Unknown Friend, there are many people who find the process of moving away from past memories very difficult indeed. They think that a new relationship may mask the pain of a previous one. They become angry or frustrated when they think about past events. They make the same mistake again, they will not attempt to learn new mind processes. We will visit the process of how to overcome this and other difficult problems many times within this book. Be clear in your mind, the whole of this book IS the process!

As you read through the book, you will find there is some repetition of ideas. This is intentional. In fact practice and repetition are the tools of learning how to do almost everything. The transformations you can make to your life do not happen overnight, but with gentle, constant and repetitional effort you can turn your lifetime into whatever you desire. I am not promising you material wealth, I promise you nothing. Read the book, use the ideas you like, discard the ideas you do not.

There is a saying, "Charity begins at home" this book guides you to be focussed in your world, as you empower your 'inner being' you will find that your relationships with others will become clearer and more defined. You are your most important friend, you are your most important being. Happiness begins in your 'inner being', do not doubt it, the words in the book revolve around YOU. You are your most important person, believe in yourself.

You will read the word 'success' many times as you go through the chapters. Let me clarify, I am not always referring to material success, success is holistic, which means a successful person is made from many successes, there will be intellectual, emotional, spiritual and material successes in every 'wholesome' person.

The success of which I write is the success of ones 'being' which allows one to say, "I have a life well lived".

Ian Timothy

www.IanTimothy.com

2. NEVER LET ANYTHING WORRY YOU

Learn to 'Never Let Anything Worry You' and you are able to become many steps nearer to the happiness called freedom. You are by my side as I write these words and I write with caution, because I would like you to be gently awakened to using rational thinking. I ask you to be open minded as you read each chapter, some you may find a little difficult to accept, as they may conflict with some of your beliefs, I know this, I understand this, yet still, I must write them.

A human is born, lives a life and then dies. Does one human experience have any real importance in the great scheme of creation? Unknown Friend we will investigate this and other ideas as we work through this little book.

Each chapter is a meditation which will provoke certain thoughts. I feel these thoughts will lead you to subtle and powerful realisations. If you wish, you could read a chapter and meditate upon the information, words, and ideas contained within it. In fact just meditating upon the name of each chapter will develop some interesting self realisations! Let me clarify again, each meditation is written to make you think deeply about, and reason with, the subject written about within each chapter. Be open minded as you think about the ideas and concepts, do not dismiss them on first reading. The chapters are written to help you to form a strong and open mind. After reading this book you may well find you have become more confident in the way you communicate, with yourself, and with those who are part of your life.

Each chapter investigates life's potentials and beliefs. I hope it guides you to becoming an empowered human being! Never be afraid to change your mind or opinion Make a few mistakes and admit to your mistakes, you will become a better person for it. If you never worry about anything, you will discover that no one nor any situation will effect you. Do not doubt the incredible power of learning how to do this.

Nothing will worry you if you learn to reason carefully and factually about any subject, the process is not an easy nor an instantaneous one. Unknown Friend, you are a human and you are made in the same way as any other human, therefore, you are able to do as well as any other. You may not be certain of this at this moment in time, that by the time you finish this book you may well have awakened your ability to begin to fulfil your potentials.

Have you ever listened to someone say, 'I only have the usual day to day worries'? What fools they are to make this statement! There is no such thing as a day to day worry. If someone has a consistent problem, they need to deal with it!

If you only meditated for a few minutes a day on the three mantras below, you would change your lifetime forever. You will learn more as we read through the book together. Yes, Unknown Friend you are in my mind as I write these words, I am with you as you read them. We are together as I write this book.

Read these phrases of empowerment. If you only said these words to yourself once a day you would improve your life beyond your wildest dreams.

"I am looking forward to my future"
"I believe in myself and my right to have my own thoughts"
"I will Never let Anything Worry Me"

3. UNIVERSE AND BIRTH

Birth is the beginning, death is the ending, every moment of a lifetime is the middle or centre. I ask you to accept that you are the centre of your lifetime and universe. We may well have not been born equal to others, we do have the same brain and body, you can listen to a man with a North American accent, you know more or less where he came from, listen to an English man, you know more or less where he came from. Their accents, their use of their language has been learnt, their attitudes were learnt, their belief system was learnt, every single part of the humans character is learnt. The psychiatrist CJ Jung called this collective conscience. His incredible mind guides you to accept the fact: "You are the sum of all your lifetime encounters, everything from your mother to a spider can effect your life!"

How big is the universe? Read this attempt of explaining the vastness of it. Just imagine one grain of sand on a beach represents the earth, and the rest of the planet represents the universe, the universe is a big space! Does your lifetime, or indeed any human who has lived upon this planet, have any significance to the universe? The probable answer is, not too much. Do you consider an ant as significant or not? I do not know if the little ant has a purpose, to me it does not matter, the ant is here by chance. I know the little ant does have a part to play in it's ant colony, as you have a part to play in your social system called the human race. You will have an important significance to yourself, your friends and family.

You exist within the universe, you do not know why the universe exists, you do not know why you exist, you are a result of chance. You are a very small part in the evolution of the universe and the universe will not change at the moment of your death The universe did not change after the deaths of all the people in the first and second world wars. Many of the stars in the sky no longer exist. The universe is not concerned, it just keeps on ticking away like a perpetual grandfather clock.

If you accept this fact, you can make a mighty fine job of living a brilliant lifetime, making each moment count, demanding freedom, refusing to encroach upon another man's domain, only fighting when someone attempts to encroach upon your own! Live your lifetime in the way of truth, so that when you go to your final sleep, you will be content if one man says about you "There is an example of a lifetime well lived"

No matter what a scientist tells us, no matter how the politician, banker, industrialist attempts to imprison us, each of us is at the centre of our universe. If we learn to culture a single minded attitude (single minded, not selfish) we discover that nothing or no one can imprison us.

Become the focal point of your lifetime, be selective, choose only that which is positive, work to enjoy freedom for yourself and demand and talk of freedom for other humans. If you compromise, you fold under the spell of the oppressor or system which attempts to steal your life hours. With the knowledge that you only have one lifetime, you must live every moment of it, you must shout this truth every time you are given the opportunity. I like to shout these words out as loud as I can "This is my lifetime, I live the journey just once, I will live every moment in truth and happiness". Believe me, Unknown Friend, I really live by those words and phrases.

Imagine how wonderful it would be if you could realise all of your potentials into realities. When clear and precise thoughts are used to plan and formulate your human experience, you are able to do so. Meditate deeply on the power of reality. When you are at the centre of your universe, you can guide yourself to have realistic thoughts and your perspective of life will gently evolve for the better.

At the centre of your universe, you can be as close as you like to another, so long as you allow that other to have their own centre of their universe. This is real freedom. I put it to you that by thinking about being at the centre of your universe, you become free and independent, and by allowing all those around you to be at the centre of their universe, you do not become distanced from each other, you actually become closer! As you focus upon your own existence and your own personal development, you will never have to think about what people think of you, because you will be the very best "being" you can be! This makes you more acceptable to others and, as a result, you have more friends not less.

The next time you look up at a clear night sky, think about these words that came to me forty years ago "Like the stars in the sky, family and friends can look so very close yet in reality, they can be so very far apart, even so, they shine like stars in my heart". How I wish I had listened to the truth of my words during my existence. The observation allows you to see you can be at the centre of your universe and still wonder at the silent inspiration of the bright stars which surround you.

You are born into a very big world. You can choose to be the centre of your universe or not. Whatever you choose, whatever you do, however you live, it will be your truth, so follow it. It matters not one jot to me if the whole world dislikes my words or ideas. I live in my truth at the centre of my universe. If I cannot follow my own truth, then surely I am imprisoned by the thoughts of others, are you imprisoned by the thought or actions of others? If you are, you are not at the centre of your universe.

At the centre of the lifetime there is a place called thought. What is thought can be created. Create a worry free universe, Unknown Friend live a 'lifetime well lived'!

4. LIVING IN THE MOMENT

This concept is of such importance I will write about it in depth. Without exception every successful person I have interviewed uses this lifetime skill. Initially we do not have to do anything, in fact the process is so potent you only need to meditate on the *why and the how* for 'The Moment' to start working for you. 'The Moment' is like a big steam train, it takes effort to get it to move, once momentum begins, it is difficult to stop. When the incredible human potential is awakened, potentials become realities, your incredible 'being' takes on the power of the steam train saying "watch out I am coming your way"

As I go through the process of writing this book every effort is put into each chapter. The book invites you to think about 'truth' 'potentials' 'the moment' it helps you to do this by introducing you to some very inspirational people.

For 35 years of my life I lived an illusion. I had good ideas that initially worked well, then they lost momentum, I did not stay in 'The Moment' therefore I was doomed to fail.

This book was written in 'The Moment' which is the best way that I know, to secure a successful future, 'The Moment' demanded I stayed focused upon the book until it was finished, all potentials can become realities which will come to fruition, if you finish what you have started. So many great plans fail at the last hurdle, never give up.

Each time a copy is purchase it is due to 'The Moment' being activated in November 2011, and focused upon to its completion in September of 2012. What does this tell you? It tells you 'The Moment' is a continuous flow of creativity which moves with you in your lifetime. Imagine the suns rays focused through a magnifying glass, move the glass forward or backward in time and it does not create the hot spot. You are the magnifying glass, keep the rays of creativity in focus!

You are at work and someone says, "I do not see why we should do this" or "This is a waste of time" they still activate 'The Moment' and it is now working against them! They are focused in 'The Moment' of failure. The process turns around immediately once the attitude becomes, "I get paid the same if I do the job well or with indifference, I will always do the job well" People see that you are working to the best of your potential. This is how, and why, some people climb the ladder of success, whilst the majority only see, the few succeed. I clarify it more in the next paragraph.

'The Moment' is interesting, when it is activated, it will keep on working and once started it is difficult to stop! 'The Moment' works for positive action and negative action. Many are lazy, many just want the easy life, many are not prepared to take time to learn, many just do not care. For these people 'The Moment' is casting a shadow into their future. They cannot change anything that they have done, they cannot turn back time and if they continue in their sloth, they cannot expect anything other that the mundane and negative world they live in.

There is no point in attempting to change any negative action. When you decide to become a positive 'being', you start by acting in a positive way, living in the truth and very quickly your positive potentials become realities! Be clear in your mind, you cannot change anything that has happened, how you react to any experience will effect your future.

Once you start drawing lines, forgiving and/or forgetting negative people or past events, you are taking your first steps to a worry free lifetime. You may well have to really push yourself and use extraordinary effort to overwhelm past methods of thinking. Never give up, you are worth the effort!

'The Moment' is so important that we should look at it from many different angles. Just think deeply about the next few paragraphs, as it is the method that matters. Do you want to be in a lifetime of reality fulfilling your potentials? If so, learn this 'truth' - the actual experience of anything that has happened to you occurred due to a series of moments, if you attempt to look back you will only see the scenery of the past, lifetime moves quickly, the past images will be distorted, the future is only an illusion or at best, a possibility. As you feed the furnace of the train called 'The Moment' you drive it into your future, everything you do at this moment will effect your future. If you constantly look back, the train slows down, because you are not working in 'The Moment'. Attempting to look too far forward? Again, the train slows down, because you are one step ahead of your self! By working effectively in 'The Moment' the train gains speed, progress then becomes swift and certain.

This example is how 'The Moment' works. A film production company comes together, a script is read, a director found, a film crew selected, actors auditioned, hours are spent rehearsing, sets are built, the filming starts, hours and hours of effort, thousands of money tokens spent, the film is made, all of the skills, time, experience, is now condensed into 120 minutes of entertainment, you watch the film, it was made in a string of moments, if they get it right, the film earns fortunes for all concerned for years and years to come. The legacy of the script (the idea, the creative thought) and the production becomes a consistent future income! If the film fails, another is made, because in the big scheme, the lessons learned will be useful in the next production. The production company knows that it will get more films right that it gets wrong, they are constantly working in

'The Moment'. Constant positive effort always succeeds in the end.

   Julie and Sandy are teachers, their story starts in 1987. At that time their combined income was 22000, they purchased a house for 45000, they wanted to pay off the mortgage quickly, so for 5 years they lived on Sandy's wage and every single penny of Julie's wage was used to pay off the mortgage. In 1992 they buy another house, this time it is 100000 (the value of the old house increased and was used as a deposit) as a result there was only 30000 outstanding on their new mortgage and their joint wages had increased. The outstanding amount was paid off in 3 years. For 8 years they worked totally in 'The Moment' dedicated to a plan.

   Sandy tells me "By 1995 we had paid for our house which is now worth a staggering 395000, we have always saved Julie's wages. With no mortgage, my wages are more than enough for our needs. In the last 10 years we have saved over 300000, Julie is paid 23000 after tax per year and 10x23 =230 thousand and there is a yearly residue from my income! by the time we retire we will be worth in excess of a million (house and savings) we will also have an excellent pension"

   Do you not think this is amazing? Two people working as teachers to one common purpose become millionaires without the slightest effort. This IS 'The Moment' at its very best. Julie and Sandy tell me, they have never spent a penny on life insurance or pension schemes preferring to pile everything into their own lifetime. They have never gone without anything. Even more interesting is that when Sandy is talking he consistently uses the binding words "our and we".

Unknown Friend, if you feed the furnace of 'The Moment' with positive thoughts and actions, you will find your own way to freedom. Feed the furnace of 'The Moment' with negative thoughts and actions and it will take you in the wrong direction. Many believe that the answers are in the past. Yes, there are lessons to be learnt. However, Unknown Friend, it is the actions of today which are lighting the road the future.

5. MANY BELIEFS

Is the way you live your life the realisation of your beliefs? When you look in the mirror do you believe what you see? Do you believe in your actions, your words, you desires, do you believe everything in your mind? Or are you living someone else's beliefs?

There are twenty-six letters in the English alphabet, and there are nine numerical symbols and a zero, you can use these letters and symbols of communication to transfer most of the thoughts which are within your mind, into the mind, of A.N. Other. The words you speak can be inaccurate (I am not writing about lies) you may be misunderstood, or the information you have may be flawed. The words you write are slightly different from the words you speak, because you can reread, research and reflect upon your written thoughts.

I invite you to write about yourself, as you are, at this moment of your life. Take your time, there is no hurry, use the chapter titles of this book to answer certain questions, What is in my universe? How much freedom do I really have? Do I respect nature? Keep on writing your book of truth and beliefs, a sentence a day, a page a day, whatever. Take your time to reread about yourself and you will find that you may begin to adapt your attitudes. Your likes and dislikes, loves and desires, the thoughts that make you happy, eliminating those that made you sad! You will not know when the changes for the better take place, yet you can be sure beneficial changes will happen!

If you agree that by using twenty-six letters, nine symbols and a zero you can communicate almost all of your wisdom and knowledge to A. N. Other (and this is an incredible realisation), you may agree that there was not a specific moment when you actually realised you could read and write. Not only this, there was not a specific moment when you realised you could talk. You have already done the three most difficult things a human needs to learn, reading, writing and speaking! I have now proven that you are as bright as anyone else.

Your mind is full of information, good, indifferent, useless and bad. You have thousands of pieces of information within it and how you combine the information forms your beliefs. It is your beliefs which make you successful or not, rich or poor, happy or sad. You did not know when you formed your beliefs, they just evolved.

You are an incredibly complex 'being' and long term change cannot 'just' happen. You need to gently coax your mind into letting positive beliefs and attitudes become the creative force, within your 'being'.

You do not usually form instantaneous beliefs. Your mind takes its time and does not like confusion. You have thousands of hours of information stored in your memory. Your beliefs take days, weeks, months and years to form in your mind.

A father says, "That tribe is evil", the son does not have the full facts, so he believes his father's words, the belief becomes so strong, that for no reason whatsoever the boy grows up to hate the tribe, he hates them so much he wants to kill them and he uses words to change the beliefs of his friends and anyone who will listen. Soon the tribes are at war, now everyone hates each other and their ingrained beliefs cause pain, upset, unhappiness. All this happens because of the belief of the father. One day the son asks his father, "Why is the tribe evil?" And sadly his father cannot remember.

The trick is to look at our life in truth and with realism, without reference to what we believe. If you are worried about anything deal with it, pick up the phone, write the e-mail, speak to the person and 'come to terms' with the problem.

Do not believe you cannot do something, just begin to do it. You may find that your beliefs are your limitations. You may not believe you cannot become free from worry,

I know this is a false belief! You may not believe you are intelligent, even though I have just proven to you that you are. The proof? You can read, write and have a conversation, the three most difficult processes any human can learn.

If you do not believe you cannot do something, ask yourself why not? Be realistic, you cannot become a doctor, dentist, lawyer without learning how to do so! To do anything you have to learn the process which makes it happen. Relationships have a process, a happy family life has a process, your job has a process, everything has a process and you have to think, study, learn and relearn how to do anything which is constantly causing distress.

Unknown Friend, If you believe you cannot do something, it is because you have not studied the process. You cannot 'just' become anything. You cannot 'just' instantaneously believe anything. Your mind is constantly cross referencing to the hundreds of other beliefs which are within your memory. Beliefs can be very limiting.

For example, there are some people I would rather not have as friends. I may not be too keen of their ethics, morals or principals, however, I can respect their work, their ability, or their achievements. I would not limit myself, my future, or my progress, by not working with someone because of my *beliefs*. I may believe in God but this would not prevent me working with an atheist. I do not believe that war solves anything but this would not prevent me from being the friend of a soldier. I do not

21

believe the slaughter of whales is for scientific purposes but I will still buy Japanese optical products.

I do not hide my beliefs, Nor should you! Be clear and transparent with your friends, family and foes. I now have a real doubt about the idea of life after death, I no longer believe that there is such a thing as a 'miracle' cure, I am seriously questioning many of my spiritual beliefs. I do not let this 'questioning' of my previously held beliefs, worry me or effect me. On the contrary, I feel this self questioning to be beneficial and progressive, I do not worry if I cannot find instant answers, *instantaneous* epiphanies may take years to form!

I listen to successful people talk about how they have succeeded in their life. I ask "Is belief a major factor in your success?" Very often they say something like, "Belief is very important, however you have to take action, you have to learn, you have to forgive, you have to move on, you have to be open minded."

Like the little boy who was told by his father "that tribe is evil" you may not know why you believe in the certain things. You will do well to investigate your beliefs, write your journal, ask people what they think *you* believe in, listen to other people's beliefs, look at how the beliefs of other people effect their lives. Beliefs can be powerful friends or treacherous enemies, choose them well.

As you question your beliefs, ask are they truthful, moral and without prejudice? Unknown Friend, the process of change can be a very difficult one if you do not accept it will take time, and if you are not careful with your thoughts and beliefs! Your quest for freedom from worry may evade you, and what a great pity this would be.

6. TIME

It's a Sunday, five thirty in the morning, I got up half an hour ago, I woke up early, went downstairs into my kitchen, from the cold water tap I poured a glass of water, filled the kettle, emptied the dish washer, unloaded the washing machine, put the damp washing into the tumble dryer, reloaded the washing machine with dirty clothes, drank the fresh water, made my coffee, I then took the bin liner out of the waste bin, took that to the garbage bin, I then feed the wild birds, they need some fresh water in their bird bath, so I clean and refill it, I go to the bottom of the garden to see how the sunflowers are getting on, I am now sitting at my desk in front of the Apple computer that earns my living, I look at my download site to find that I have sold some of my work, I then look at my web site to discover I have sold some CDs, I have a number of emails to read and a few to answer.

I now look at the time it is six thirty, I drink another glass of water, make another cup of coffee and read through what I have just typed. Later in the day if the weather is good, I will cut the grass and hedges, cook a really nice afternoon meal, as the day comes to an end I will sit in the garden with Lizzy and smoke a pipe of tobacco, drink a couple of glasses of wine, then retire to bed to watch a film that is streamed down from the internet (I do not have a television, I love watching old films)

What a fortunate man I am, 54 years of age, I know I am fortunate, read the first paragraph again. I have a supply of clean fresh water in my kitchen, I have clean fresh clothes to wear, I have access to a healthy sanitation system, I have a thriving and happy community of wild birds as my pets, Lizzy and I can grow sunflowers instead of having to grow food (although this may change in time) I earn my living from my creative ability, I can communicate with my friends and customers from all over the world, At this moment I am drinking coffee from Brazil, this afternoon I will eat some lamb which came from New Zealand, this evening I will smoke some tobacco which was grown in America and drink some red wine that came from Italy, I will finish my day by being able to have a hot shower and sit in my bed being able to watch film because of the miracle called the internet. No one can dispute that I truly live in an incredible world. You live in this incredible world too!

Unknown Friend, as you now know, the past does not exist and the future is just in front of you. You know that your actions of the moment cascade into your future, so your actions and thoughts manifest your future. Today I have planned to cook some food, work in my garden, etc, but what would happen if a friend called and said he was coming to see us? The whole day would change. I would walk into town in order to buy some extra wine and food, then I would relax, talk, enjoy the hours with my friend. All could change in a moment and I am ready and adaptable, nothing that occurs worries me, I live my life and take advantage of the best options that come my way. I know that time is my most valuable asset and I intend to use that asset as much as I possibly can.

What do we learn from the first few paragraphs, you will read elsewhere that once I had depression, nine years ago I had little money and very few friends, I was in a difficult place of my own making, I now live a fantastic life, no debt, worries or problems, I have achieved this just by making each and every moment add up into a wonderful life, I have achieved this by not putting a value on anything of a material nature and putting a real value on honesty, friendship, love, my wellbeing, happiness and valuing every single second of my existence. If I can do this, anyone can.

Unknown Friend, if you work diligently to enjoy every moment that you live, have the wisdom not to waste too much of your life in front of a television or any other futile distraction, understand that you have to put effort into your life to reap the harvest of your endeavours, become devoted to your hopes and inspirations, have the discipline to remove negative people, situations, opinions from your life, love the beauty of nature and fellow humans, make the correct choices though clear and rational thinking, educate yourself in as many ways that you can, remove the egotistical attitudes of the majority then you will walk into a future full of good fortune and happiness.

Last night we went to a wedding reception. It was a very nice evening, I have a slight headache because I drank just a little too much! There were many people there, I enjoyed their company. I love meeting new people and when they ask me the inevitable question "what do you do?" I always answer "enjoy my life" this always confuses them and they reply "no, what do you DO for a living?" "enjoy my life" is my answer, at that point they either walk away because they think I am being difficult, or they try to get more information from me. I want to be listening to them, I want to know about them, so I tell them, "You are my living, all people are my living, I learn from people, I write about what I learn, I look at people and I photograph their images, I talk to people and make films about them, that is what I do and I love it" very quickly they begin to tell me about their own interesting lives. Everyone has an interesting life, many do not think so, and how wrong they are! Very often I will hear the statement "if only I had more time" someone told me this last night.

I was introduced to "Olin" who within minutes told me she owned a business which had been through difficult times and now generated a lot of money. Olin lives in a very big house, drives a very expensive car and is totally engrossed in her business, when I asked her what she did for a hobby or interest, the inevitable reply was she has no time to do anything like that! can you relate to Olin? Do you know someone like Olin? Who is so wrapped up in the material world they "have no time" to do anything? Success is her objective, her life, her reason, did the trappings of the success fulfil her life? I have no idea. Two times during the conversation she went outside to smoke a cigarette, on the third time she did not come back, I felt that she was somewhere else, lost in her own world, with a need to tell anyone who would listen, about her successful business, she has many 'Unknown Friends' who will know her very well indeed.

Why do I introduce you to Olin? It must be obvious. I ask you to reflect upon the ratio of work to recreation. Are the hours put into a material objective worth the price it demands?

The time is now eight thirty. There is a lovely blue sky outside. I will have another cup of coffee, I am going to start my day in a moment! Because I have got the time to do the things I want to do, I am not going to waste a moment of it. Make sure Unknown Friend, you do not waste any more of yours. Every single second is precious. If you understand this you will learn that to worry is wasting your time.

7. LIFE

'Life is not a test. Life is the learning and education which will bring happiness to our 'being'' ~ Ian Timothy.

You are the result of a chance in time, a physical connection between two people, if your egg had been lost in your mothers cycle, you would not exist. If you accept this fact, it guides you to many realisations.

There are many who teach that a spirit or soul chooses to become a human to "go through" certain life experiences. Did six million souls really decide to experience mass destruction as Jews between 1939-1945? Did 200 million souls choose to die in terrible pain during the wars of the last 2000 years? Millions by starvation? etc. Oh! It's a pointless task attempting to rationalise the concept of a soul or spirit choosing a life experience.

Karma? Stalin murdered millions of Russians and died of natural causes. People break many forms of the one sin and the lawyer gets them off on a point of law. Drug dealers sell death and poverty and live like kings. An atom bomb created, evil weapons devised and the scientist receives a prize paid for from the production of dynamite. A kind and wonderful friend is diagnosed with MS. How far do you want to go with the concept of karma? I have no idea if karma exists, if it does, its not too convincing.

The only journey I have ahead of me is my lifetime and my objective is to experience as much happiness and freedom as possible. I do not need poorly thought out spiritual concepts to worry me or cause confusion within my lifetime. Fate, destiny, pre-determined life and karma? Ask yourself if they are excuses.

I am talking to Ruth "I am having a terrible time at the moment, I cannot find a job, my partner is spending too much money on cannabis, the neighbours are playing music every moment of the day and night, I am praying to God, He is not listening, Is this happening to me because of something I have done in this life or in another life? am I being affected by *karma?*" she asks "No, you cannot find a job because you are tired, have too much pride to do any type of job, you consider low paid work is beneath you, your partner is a waster who uses drugs, you have not got enough money to move out of the neighbourhood you are living in, Ruth you are making poor lifetime choices and you are paying the price, you may call it *Karma*, I call it lack of responsibility"

"What can I do" she asks? My answer " No one has ever received a cheque from God, An inherent creative force gives every human the same facilities and opportunities, I know that many are born at a disadvantage which will be difficult or impossible to overwhelm. Accept this fact Ruth, do any job, do not do nothing, put your whole "being" into that job, live like a church mouse, save some money to move to a better place, the waster you have as a partner needs to shape up or go, you may tell me you love him, does he love you? He constantly spends your money on drugs, he is lazy, he is filthy, he stinks, he is bringing you down, you are being dammed by your association with this bum" Ruth turned around and walked away.

Lifetime is what you make it. A creative force is freely available to each of us. I ask you to draw from this well of abundance. This force takes on many guises, your job, your family, your friends, your garden, your body, your thoughts, your mind, your relationships, are all creative forces. Ultimately it is how you control your lifetime and how much effort you put into your lifetime that decides your future.

Your creative force is at its greatest in times of stillness. When you are in stillness or silence you will start a process, which will turn a potential into a reality. If things are not going well for you, stop, think and settle down the mind. Put yourself at the centre of your universe. Think about the truth. Realise you may have to make a sacrifice or two (in the old days they set their favourite cow on fire)! These days, you may have to sell a few possessions, set up a re-payment plan, work some overtime, cut up the credit cards. If you formulate a silent plan and then act upon it,

31

you will bring your life back on track. Life is for living, and one should approach it with a sensible and factual attitude.

You are living in the so called modern world, and this modern world can be tough. You could be living in a moment of oppression, for example, an excess of work for little return. A feeling one '*must*' have a family, because that is what is expected, one *must* have a big house, because that shows the world how brilliant you are. Or you may be very sensible, understanding that working in the present 'moment' will allow the fantastic future to unfold before you.

I personally recommend a responsible attitude towards work, lots of walking, travel, exercise, good food, friends, no debt, a small glass of wine now and again and everything will shape up just dandy! You may become as happy as me by following a totally opposite path! Life's options and choices are wonderfully expansive, sometimes testing. Use them to your advantage. Even making the wrong choice or taking the wrong option can eventually be seen as incredibly enlightening and beneficial, I have not got time to waste by worrying about mistakes! I have a lifetime to live! Some more mistakes to make! I am not going to worry about anything. Creative force, deal me another hand of experiences, I have my lifetime at stake and I am only going to gamble on what I can afford to lose!

There are those who live from charity when they are perfectly able to provide for themselves, they will find every excuse not to be responsible for their lifetime, they receive just one hand of cards at the table of existence. Lets hope they can see there are some very sharp players at the table who play for high stakes. You will do well to understand that the card sharps of life will take the lazy players stakes, without a second thought.

There are not many short cuts that actually work. Most direct roads to happiness and success take time to build. Effort, setback, laughter, dark days, happy days are all part of the construction of your lifetime. The often heard statement "That's life, my friend" is a powerful acknowledgement of the way life really is.

Life has a beginning, it has an end, make the middle as interesting as possible. If the centre of your existence called lifetime has not been so good up to this point, shift the beginning to TODAY and start your life again. Why? Because anyone who has said, "Where has my life gone?' has realised that TIME is their most valuable asset. The clock of your available time whispers "tick…I am only wound up once…tock"

This is not the first place in the book that I write upon the concept of 'living in the moment'. I remind you again, if you live in the moment, make every action and thought, right, bright and positive, you will form a future which will become incredibly enriching, Those who choose to live in negativity, moan, find fault, think badly of others will find their lifetime a difficult and exhausting process.

Ian Timothy

Life is a journey of experiences, some good, some bad. Life can be blissful or hard. Whatever it is, you are well advised to live it to the full, with no regrets, no hard luck stories. Think about this, when you are at your last moment, your clock will say.."tick…I am only wound up once…tock…I told you so"…then silence.

And Ruth? She works in a coffee shop, has a new partner, a new apartment in a nice part of the city, I am told she is saving to own her own cafe. She has never spoken to me since our last conversation. Does this worry me? No, I do not bear false witness, I speak my truth. Life is too short to analyse the past.

8. CONSCIENCE

There is only one sin, it is called theft. If you kill a man you steal his life, lie to him you steal his truth, take his car you steal his property, persecute him you steal his freedom, bully him you steal his dignity. Unknown Friend, there is only one sin.

I cannot guide you to what is right or wrong, some of us have high values, some have very few. There are hundreds of ideas of what is good and what is bad. There is only one rule of life which clearly states 'thou shalt not steal'.

When we enter the nursery of the mind, the toys you can play with are rules, emotions, thoughts, tastes, smells, words, learnings, everything that is needed to form your personality and character is available to you. One of the most powerful toys in the box is called our conscience, it is like a kind messenger or a loud siren, warning you that you need to think carefully about your actions, towards yourself, and towards others.

We can falsely believe that we have hurt someone when we have not, the smallest situation can cause discord. We need to look at this in perspective because an inaccurate assessment of our actions towards others can be one of the biggest setbacks in a quest to become free from worry.

If you are in doubt, if you feel you have offended another, ask if you have offended, find out if you have caused hurt, realise the truth, and then apologise if needed or breath a sigh of relief! If you feel guilty due to your own actions toward yourself, then I am afraid you will have to change the action which is causing you guilt. This may take time and constant effort, making changes often demands that we have to invest a lot of time and effort into our desired outcome. We may have to start over many times before the journey is completed.

No one, should have any guilty feelings if what they have said about any subject is accurate or true. I repeat, you can be certain of this fact, if what you are saying or doing is accurate and true, there is no cause for your conscience to become active. Again the principal of clear and precise thought wins the day in the quest for a worry free life.

In the nursery of your mind, there is a toy box full of memories, ideas, principals, facts, illusions, and with those toys, you can construct anything! And one of the main 'things' you construct is your belief's. 'A' belief is constructed in *your* mind, it is only an idea, it is only *your* idea. It is important that you really think about this next sentence, as it will help to free you from feeling unnecessary guilt. Remember your belief of a subject is rarely exactly the same as another person's belief of the same subject. Do not allow the opinions of other people, in regard to the way you live your life, make you feel guilty for what you have done.

You could feel guilty about the food you have eaten, smoking, having a flirtatious conversation with a stranger, not putting enough in the collection box, chilling out when the lawn needs cutting, buying a glass of wine when you are a little short of money. You may even feel guilt if you do not have any problems (this is because you feel you are not doing enough) you could feel guilty because you became angry with a loved one, the list is endless.

We can feel ill at ease due to many things, which are in actual fact, of no importance at all. Guilt is a very restrictive emotion, it is fine and cautionary if it is part of a clear thinking mind but it is restrictive and destructive if it is part of a fogged mind.

Here comes the past again! There may be a memory of a negative action, which you have done or said to another or to yourself, and this memory could make you feel guilty. How do you deal with it?

The simple and only answer is to forgive yourself or anyone for anything that has caused upset in your life. If you are unable to do this, you are restricting your future

37

and sooner or later you will have to move on or become bitter or unhappy.

Unknown Friend, Forgiveness and apology are the words we all know the meaning of, if you cannot forgive, then forget and move on. If you have done something to another which you feel is wrong, if you have done something to yourself that you know is wrong, close it down, work around it, live in the moment, forgive, forget and apologise. You are not the person today, that you were yesterday, we all make mistakes.

You cannot think about two things at one time, when any negative thought comes into your mind, overcome it with a positive one, and keep on doing this until it becomes your way of thinking. Initially you will not find this too easy, stay with it, because you will train your mind to be what you want it to be. I can prove this to you. By telling you, that you have trained your mind to be who you have become *NOW* train your mind to be who you want to be, and your conscience will be clear.

9. EDUCATION

Unknown Friend, the mind needs to be educated throughout it's lifetime. I am not writing about teachings or lessons of formal education, although this is something well worth considering, I guide you towards searching and looking for factual information which will serve you well.

Again and again I will guide you to write notes and keep a journal, I am always making notes and even if they seem strange at the time they are written, they are important to my thinking process. I ask you to seek the company of intelligent people. I am very fortunate, I know a lot of very astute thinkers! If you cannot find some locally, go world wide join a forum on the internet. My goodness there are some very fast minds in the world, contact them, talk to them, listen to them.

You may spend small fortunes on self help books which fail in their objective. When you learn to think and reason, with clarity, you probably give yourself more of an advantage than any formal degree could! You will be on the road to successes beyond your wildest dreams.

The young man or woman who takes a university degree often fails to become successful in their field of study, the historian becomes a manager of a supermarket, the architect becomes a boat builder, the psychologist becomes an hotelier, and even though they are worlds apart from their degree, they still become incredibly successful.

Why is this? Because their higher education taught them to think, no more or no less they learnt to reason, they learnt to research information and use it. That is why any one who learns to reason and think has an advantage over those who use 'gut' feelings or take chances.

Some of those who take chances or go with their 'feelings' may find incredible success, sadly they are a minority. On a material level the bankruptcy courts are full of those who take the chances and fail, and do not make any mistake you could well experience more failures than successes if you allow, the 'calculated risk' to become part of your game plan.

The incredible successes of a very, very, small minority are used by many writers of the 'the ways to riches' books and very often the authors have not the slightest idea of what it takes to be successful. I am a reasonably successful man and my goodness the journey has been a tough one, my success has taken 35 years of hard lessons, learnt in the very hardest ways.

I have come to the conclusion that there is very little difference in the way we achieve success, the process is much the same, effort, discipline, truth, integrity, planning, good friends, family, love, desire, and kindness work every time in our personal life and in the advancement of one's career.

Educate your mind to become free of worry. If I had discovered 4 books before my 20th birthday I would have saved myself 35 years of failures! These books are:

'Man's Search for Meaning' by Victor Frankl
'The Richest Man in Babylon by George Samuel Clason
'Jonathan Livingstone Seagull' by Richard Bach
'As Man Thinketh' by James Allen

Each of these books contain the jewels in a crown worn only by those who really taste the riches of real success. My goodness if you followed the words of those authors to the letter you would have a doctorate of life before your name.

I do not write of revisiting formal education, you may well be lacking in determination to do this. The world is full of mature students who achieve a degree late in life (this IS a wonderful and inspiring thing to do) and do nothing with their degree. I am sure it is the feeling of incredible achievement which brings as much pleasure to them as the degree itself. I write in the hope that you kindle a desire to re-educate yourself in any way, I assure you this one act will open your mind to expansive and opinion changing ideas.

You could start your re-education by reading the books I have mentioned, they are not expensive. Victor's book is a mind expanding read, George's book is the way to material comfort, James's book is the book of reality, Richard's book is the book of independence. Individually they make you think, if you combined the wisdom they hold within you could become a professor of truth.

I know these books well. When I interview people and listen to the ways some of them easily succeed or why some have had to fight long and hard to find their freedom, I am often reminded of how powerful the words written within those books really are, as those who succeed in life seem to use the principals that are found within their pages. There is no point attempting to reinvent the wheel. Victor, George, James and Richard have done the work, read their books!

Try not to fall into the trap of the millions who just exist and live in some hope that a 'life well lived' will just happen as if by magic! They seem to believe in an illusion, that if they desire something so very much the 'Universe' will provide whatever they want. They educate themselves in false hopes and pipe dreams learnt from the 'professors' of greed and deception. Let me dispel one of the guru's distorted spells. There is no secret of the universe which will bring wealth, happiness and success to you. Only your efforts, the sweat of your brow and learning the right processes and method of success, will bring you success!

I will make you feel a little uncomfortable for a few moments. I do this to help you to realise that to only think about needing something, will not make it happen.

You are hungry, thirsty and in poverty. All around you there were wealthy men and women who own large cars, beautiful houses and have never experienced real hunger, your desire for food, health and warmth is without doubt greater than their desire for the illusion of wealth. Surely the universe could get them to feed you?

You are a little child who has just seen your father killed and your mother raped by soldiers, your mind screams out in a way that no man in a civilised world could ever know, your desire for freedom and release from this real hell is greater than any other. Surely the universe would free you?

You will never get anything just by praying for it, thinking about it, hoping it will happen, you will never receive a cheque from God. The only way you will get anything in life is to educate yourself to learn the right method or process and then take action. In other words, use learnt skills and work.

Do not fool yourself. there is more to education than a room full of books. If you educate yourself to be clear thinking, if you educate your mind to have realistic desires, if you educate yourself to face real truths, if you educate yourself to follow your true path, then you will begin to realise your own potentials and when you have educated yourself, you can silently educate others to help the little children we have just attempted to become.

Will you educate yourself *how* to be free from worry?

10. CHOICE

Success grows from effort and choice, not from predetermined destiny, hold this truth in you heart. Choice NOT chance formulates your future. Unknown Friend, it is a certain fact, if you *learn* to make wise choices, your choices will consistently bear fruit and you will experience the "truth" which is "freedom of choice"

During the writing of this book I made a choice which I felt would make a huge difference to my life. I decided to stop drinking alcohol every day. Those who know me, know that I really enjoy red wine or a glass of malt whisky. I felt the time had come to really restrict my alcohol intake. There were a number of factors involved, my weight, my health, my wellbeing, and the desire to turn a habit into an object! Let me explain.

I wanted to buy a new bike, I had choices to make, should I tap into my banked life hours called savings, or should I convert one pleasure into another? In other words should I undertake the spiritual exercise of sacrifice? The conversion of alcohol into a bike! Lets consider that choices sometimes require sacrifices. Lets consider that the act of sacrifice can be giving up a pleasure or something one likes (in this case alcohol) in order to achieve a certain goal, this can be incredible exercise of self discipline and therefore very beneficial to us. Lets consider that by being patient we learn self control, we value the objective of the choice and we will receive an incredible life lesson. Unknown Friend, you may wish to consider that the act of sacrifice is one of the exercises you can use to empower the way you think! Sacrifice and determination are companions you should encourage into your lifetime! I choose to sacrifice alcohol to buy my bike, this is an example of a good choice.

Choices are really powerful life development tools, because even if the choice does not turn out to be the best we could have made, there will in any event be a lesson learnt.

The system of lending effects so very many people. I was once told by a young lady "debt is a social requirement to the success of the modern world, without debt the system would collapse" she believed this and I have no doubt there are millions of others who think in this way. How can uncontrolled debt be a beneficial part of the social system? Her words guide you to realise a certain fact, people use selective thought throughout their lifetimes, some add to their burden of debt in this way, they are near the limit of their resources, they think they need a car, a watch, a half weeks wages meal. To buy the short term luxury, they buy into long term debt. Is this an example of a bad choice?

Think of something you want, be sensible, now think about the sacrificial choices, no fast food, no bottled water, no wine every night, no meals out (the list is endless) and think about these sacrifices as the price of the desire. How long would your sacrifice be for, before you OWNED your desire? How about having the desire to pay off all your debts? By not eating fast food, drinking bottled water, sodas, excessive whatever? Is this an example of a good choice?

Forget the excuse "I will buy it because I am worth it". All material choices can have a long term impact upon your freedom and wellbeing. I am not saying if you have a level head, a secure job, a solid and progressive life style that you should not enjoy everything that life has to offer. Rather, I am asking you to look at the choices you make with careful reference to past outcomes. By doing this you will have a great chance of making the right choice almost every time. If you want to take chances, be prepared to learn from your mistakes.

How we choose our life style, possessions, relationships, friendships is a constant learning process. Read about Philip and his friend Daniel.

"I was becoming disillusioned with my life, I had a good job, I still have the same one, it is hard work with great rewards. At the end of each year I have made progress, a large mortgage, no problem, my job can

47

support it, a very expensive social life, I could support that too. When I reflected upon my personal life I was just treading water, there really was something missing. Most weekends my wife and I would gather for some social activity with groups of people who were in our social class, and at one of these gatherings my life changed, I was listening to two of my friends laughing about someone I knew who had lost his job, and was in serious difficulties, they were actually taking pleasure from another man's misfortune, I asked myself was I like this? I excused myself and my wife from the party, when we got home I told her I was going to visit Daniel the very next day, she smiled, walked over to me, kissed me and told me she loved me, nothing more was said. The next day I walked the mile or so to Dan's house. As I approached it, I saw the "for sale" sign and the old ford car which had replaced the BMW. As I walked to the door, it open as if by magic, there was Dan, big smile on his face, he welcomed me in, poured me a cup of coffee"

"Great to see you, how are the family" he asked
"Fine, hows it going"?
"No problem, you see the house is for sale, it is priced to sell I will have a good surplus after the sale, Jay is working for the first time in years and loving it, I am stacking shelves at WalMart and it's ok."

"Dan did not want to talk about the job loss, he just said it was just circumstance, it was his future he needed to protect, the house was going to be sold as he could not support the repayments and the so called repayment insurance was not worth a light. Dan told me that when the house was sold he was going to rent for a few months and see what happened, he had no worries, no debts at that time and he did not intend to get any! I walked home inspired by my friend and disillusioned with the two people whose conversation I had listened to the day before.

I said to my wife, we should ask Dan and Jay over for a day, we did, our friendship grew, we started walking, camping, learnt to sail a boat, we travelled all over the states on our vacations, we enjoyed our life, our friendship, we still do. Dan took a job in a bike store, three years later he had two stores of his own. This incredible man faced his problem, made difficult choices, followed a true path, and came through the ordeal. He was smiling all the way. I learnt so much from him, and his choices inspired me to make very big changes to my life too"

Unknown Friend, as you learn to make the right choices in your life, your actions will inspire others. Meditate upon the powerful effect you can have upon another just by being observed, if you make the right choices, realise your truths, you will become a shining light who guides others just like Dan inspired Philip. Make the right choice to take your right, to be free from worry.

11. MASTER TEACHERS

I once read a book proving that Jesus did not exist. In fact the author (whose name I have forgotten) apparently wrote other books on this subject, surely one was enough? In the fullness of time I was asked my opinion about this concept, I answered in this way.

"I do think a religious master called Jesus existed, in truth it does not matter if he existed or not, I believe the messages of Jesus are incredible in their perception and power"

There are millions of people who love the teachings of his representations of love, kindness and hope, who worship the principals and the irrevocable truths that he talked of. Can we ignore the statements "turn the other cheek" (Matthew 5:39), "do not worry about the future" (Matthew 6:34), "do unto others" (Matthew 7:12), "keep on asking" (Luke 11:9-10)?

The statements in the last paragraph should stand the test of time. Do you *believe* the words are as valid now as they were 2000 years ago? The word BELIEVE is the really important factor here. If you believe the words of the Masters, then you may have found another way of dealing with some of the difficult circumstances we all encounter during our lifetime. You do not have to be religious to follow the wise and empowering words and teachings of the Spiritual Masters. Their words are really nothing more than self help guidelines which can be used to enrich our lives. Use common sense though, some old teachings have outmoded or outdated ideas which stem from ignorance or, even worse, the desire to control as their hidden message.

When the old nomadic tribes crossed the desert, they knew how to navigate from oasis to oasis. If one of their brothers strayed off the path and was lost, it was explained "They were being punished for their mortal sins". They were told there were demons in the desert which awaited to take away those who did not follow the right path in life! This was the only way that the old tribes could explain many of the situations that happened to them. They explained the unexplainable as "The will of G-d". The world over, Gods and Deities were used to explain anything that could not be explained. People lived in fear of this hidden force that could hand out pain, disease, natural disaster as a punishment to any man or tribe who broke the sin of theft. Eventually it was realised this fear could be used to control millions of people. This is how it worked: If you break the rules "I" have created as God's word, you will be punished, and the sinner will not have to wait for the demons or God to punish him, "I" will do it in God's name.

We have to use caution when we encounter many modern self proclaimed teachers, gurus, Spiritual Masters, who believe they receive or 'channel' (oh! How I dislike this word in this context) messages from Angels, Jesus and God. Unfortunately there is no central cohesion to their words. Conversations with the Creator? Doubt enters my mind. Writing fairy tales for profit? That's more like it!

We are born, we die, in between there is a lifetime. If you do not break 'the rules', if you live by 'the law' and attempt to live the 'path of truths', then you will experience real freedom and ensure that the memory of your lifetime will become an example of a 'life well travelled'. The Spiritual Masters' words can guide us to the positive principals, which we can use as a foundation on which to build a strong mind.

You could consider this example. The Japanese optical companies did not become the best camera makers in the world by inventing the camera, they looked at the best cameras in the world, then improved upon them! We are given some of the best rules of life by the Masters, you can use these fountains of wisdom to help you to formulate your own way to happiness.

From my observations of those who have a 'lifetime well travelled' I discovered they accept everything for what it is! To them, the observations and realisations which many find disagreeable, are part of life. They also accept that change for the better will happen, although the change will be very slow, they have faith in their inner being. They know War is wrong. Starvation is wrong. Theft is wrong. Terror is wrong. Racism is wrong. Global warming is wrong. They do not get angry and breed hatred, nor do they fight against these injustices. They talk and think with truth and integrity, knowing that their words do have a real and subtle effect upon those who listen.

Robert is a *passive* activist. "I often talk about what I feel is morally right, many people say to me, 'Bob I know where you are coming from, but there is nothing we can do about it'. You know the type of situation Ian, the local council cuts back on road repairs, and the mayor and six of the council go on a fact finding trip to China. Ian, in my business life I am accountable for what I do with my clients' money, those who look after public money should also be accountable for how it is used, so I follow my beliefs and I write to them, and if more people did so, there would be a change. I am not a religious man but I do believe that many of the moral teachings and wisdom contained in the good books have been well tested and proven to work, they give me a direction in my family and business life. I accept that the world is a different place to when the books were written and that's fine by me, but people do not seem to have any principals any more, probably because of poor teaching, the spiritual teacher can teach so much to those who are lost". Robert is a very successful business man. I am not surprised, he is a man who lives by some of the moralistic principals taught by the Spiritual Masters.

Ian Timothy

During our lifetime we all should write at least one letter to a politician, choose your words carefully, write of what you want for the world and its population, as you write it, think, about the Masters and the sacrifices they made, think about the planet, think about the civilians who are being murdered in the wars of so called freedom, think about the real injustices. It seems to me the so called leaders are not listening to what the people really want, they have become fixed in their determination to destroy the spirit and soul of every individual who lives a "lifetime". As you write your letter, let the words become your manifesto of truths. Do not think your efforts will be wasted, they will not be, because you will know, that you have at least attempted to remind those who attempt to govern us, of the right path to follow.

Search out the words of the Spiritual Masters, and you can easily find many of their quotations, most are worth deep contemplation. Can the Spiritual Masters heal the body? (There are many who believe illness starts in the mind.) I sense good food, keeping fit, getting lots of rest AND truthful thinking works as well. Blind faith, can be a poor option to take.

Unknown Friend, many of lessons of the Spiritual Masters have a place in the modern world, just thinking about the words they have spoken are very often a powerful way of freeing yourself from worry.

12. RESPECT FOR NATURE

Have you ever sat peacefully in a garden? I often do. I sit on a very old bench, sometimes smoking a Havana cigar, always sipping a glass of red wine or drinking a strong cup of coffee. I love these moments of contemplation. I am in my heaven.

I look around my garden, I attempt to understand nature. Consistently I realise that, no matter how much I tend the garden, no matter how many times I cut the grass, prune the flowers, weed the borders, nature just continues to do it's work. We can cultivate a garden or a vegetable patch and the moment we neglect it, nature takes over. It does not matter what man does to the planet, to a garden, to a forest, we can build a road, build a town that becomes a city, but without constant care and maintenance, nature awaits to take it all back.

This is the way it is. You can sit in your garden, you can cultivate it, you can grow the most beautiful flowers, you can grow vegetables. However, the moment you stop with the intervention of cultivation, nature will take over and the garden will return back to it's natural state, in time trees will grow, the trees turn to woods, the woods to forests.

Man can cultivate cereals, vegetables, fruits, he can harvest the seas and the pastures, he can try his utmost to harness the natural world, and this natural world awaits, in it's perfected harmony to fill the earth with trees, flowers, plants of every description, and then repopulate the planet with an abundance of animals, and all of the plan of this ecological system lays silently in every plant, animal and fish.

So it is with your mind. You can become a genius and old age will slow down your ability to think, you can look after your body and the progress of time will weaken you. There is no escape from this inevitable progress, the natural flow of time and progression of life will take you to an inevitable destination.

The human can play every move in the game of existence but the natural world cannot be changed from its path, it just follows the pattern of design that nature provides for every occurrence, insects, parasites, reptiles, fish, birds, bacterial microbes, trees, wind, rain, atoms, electrons, clouds, the sun, the planets, plants, the universe! The list endless, never ending, all life on the planet exists without a nod of the head to the most dangerous inhabitant, the human.

You can oppose nature's processes, you can fight against them, the whole of mankind can fight against nature, we will never overwhelm it, we will never change it, it has no master, it masters you. Respect it, love it, care for it.

The observation of nature tells us one thing. It tells us that to worry about anything is futile. Natural progression will always be the best way. Never rush to your objectives, learn each facet of your chosen job, hobby, skill, slowly and with certainty. Learn to follow your natural rhythms, try to progress quickly by going slowly! Progress through life in a gentle, fruitful and positive way, go with the natural flow and you will blossom in every way.

In the same way you have your natural nature, you have your inner being, you possibly fight against it, you may not even recognise it. I do not know you Unknown Friend, you are the only person who needs to know yourself. May I be so bold as to suggest the natural nature of mankind is to be happy, free of worry and free to have one's own thoughts and ideas and these freedoms produce creative and beneficial harmony to the inner 'being'. Meditate upon your personality, your character, your own temperament, you own nature.

Each thing you do, do it well, one objective at a time. Just as each tree grows in a forest, each blade of grass grows in a pasture, each animal reproduces, without any other reason than to follow the patterns of nature, find and follow your nature in the great scheme. It matters not what it is, you could walk a pilgrimage, you could become a teacher, you may drive a truck, you may become a lawyer, so long as it is good and right, you will have made your contribution to the human race and you will never have to worry about anything else.

Learn to respect the lessons of nature by observing it and think of the ways that nature can guide you to happiness. Many believe they have no purpose or reason for their existence. Compared to what? Compared to the successful celebrity? Royalty? Politician? All are only humans, all have their own personality, are they what they seem to be? I doubt it. You may desire a child and fail to conceive, you may wish to be rich and be as poor as a church mouse, you may want to be famous and be anonymous. I assure you that if you become at one with your natural nature, you will never crave for any thing, you will accept your natural 'being'.

How do you do this? Look after your most valuable possession (your body), think clearly about every action, decision, teach your head to rule your heart, follow your natural life pattern, free yourself from petty arguments, and those who wish to go against your inner desires or happiness, test your intuition, work to eliminate all that restricts your natural progression upon this earth. Consider yourself as a gardener who tends your body, conscious thoughts and actions.

You are your purpose. Know and understand that you cannot and will not be able to oppose the forces of nature. The patterns of nature are consistent, ever flowing, unbeatable. Follow your *natural nature* with patience, simplicity and courage. The human inevitably has to follow in the design of nature. At this moment in time there are many who believe that they can harness or change nature. You enhance your potential to be free from worry if you realise the forces of nature are within you, these forces will assist you on your journey.

You may ask what is your natural nature? I answer the question this way. Take the time to sit and just gently think. You may think about a tree growing, a lion relaxing in the sun, the moon, the sun or the life giving power of a glass of water and then gently think about your body, your mind and the gentle rhythm of your body. Realise or accept your body 'just is', realise or accept you 'just are' that is all. You live because you do. You are here because you are. You think because you can. No more no less, that is the way of nature.

13. FRIENDSHIP

I worked with someone who was always asking why she could never have a stable relationship. The answer was that she had very low moral standards. That was her choice. The difficulty was that everyone knew of her dilemma as she told everyone who was prepared to listen about her exploits. As time went by, fewer and fewer people were happy in her company. One day she asked me what she could do to make her life happy, my answer was "tell no one about your past, and start again" as she began to tell me why she was like she was, I stopped her "I am not interested, you are making yourself unhappy, take a good look at what is making you unhappy, self harm, followed by self pity, then hoping someone will feel sorry for you, is your way of life, it does not seem to be working very well, try taking pride in yourself, try to exercise some self control, I have no personal opinion of or about you, I have no more to say" I met her in 2011 and she was married with a beautiful daughter. "How are you"? I asked "New life, new beginnings, total happiness" she replied, smiled and walked away. She now had the future she had always really wanted which was all that mattered to her. What a beautiful person she had become.

I have many friends. I truly love them all. I have my favourite friends, I love them to the same degree but I prefer to be in their company, this is one of my truths. My friends know that I live my lifetime in truth. I have many friends because of my way of life. My friends know, I am my best friend, they know I love myself before any other, they know I will say "No" if I have to, they know that I love my partner more than them! How do they know this? Because I live by my truth.

I sometimes tell people, *they* are their most important friend, they should learn to become someone they can love and care about, they should say no when they need to, they should love their family more than me, they should live in truth. I have so many friends because I live my lifetime in my own way and freedom, not possession, is my gauge of success.

There will be people who do not like me, I am not paranoid, I know this and it suits me. I like the balance. I have no problem with the people who dislike me. I do not have to please anyone, why should I be all things to all men? I have no concern for those who do not care for me, they cannot harm me, they cannot damage me, the happiness I receive from my known friends, the pleasure I receive from my unknown friends, far outweighs the concerns others have about me! In fact, I control them, as you control those who dislike you, because to dislike someone you have to think about them in a negative way and negative thoughts are extremely damaging. Therefore, if someone does not like you and has negative thoughts toward you they are damaging their lifetime. In fact, to a small degree, you control them.

I do not entertain any negative thoughts toward anyone, it is a waste of time and damaging. I could speak a truth, for example, I could say "the politician lies" "he did not fulfil his obligation" but I do not. I am not interested in the type of individual who could possibly have a negative effect upon my 'being'. I have no concern for them, I am indifferent to them, they do not control me. My freedom is my objective. My happiness creates my truths, my beliefs, my friends, my positive outlook and attitude. These are the only attributes of life that matter! And, I know that one genuine friend will overwhelm a million enemies.

There was a time when I had another type of friend, my attraction to them was my generosity at the bar! I came into very hard times, the penny finally dropped, I took control, I picked up my mobile phone, when the deletions ended, I was left with 3 numbers. The only people who had offered me help in my time of need. Never worry about having to help those you love, although there will be a point when you have to encourage a good friend to take responsibility for their life, you will never have to worry about losing a real friend.

In my interviews I ask people "Who are your friends?" Here are some of the answers I have received "You only have two friends, your shadow and your back pocket" "a friend is just someone who is" "a friend is a place of peace and safety" "I do not trust friends any more" "you are better off without them" "a friend listens and does not judge" "my friends are my life" "I am blessed to be surrounded by them" "my family are all the friends I will ever need".

The choice of friends can "make or break" you as a human "being". Work to free yourself from those with negative opinion and attitude. This action will renew your "inner force". This positive act will attract you to those who are also of a positive, progressive nature. It is usually the case that those who think in negative ways and harbour negative thoughts are manifesting failure within their lifetime. Align yourself with winners not losers! There are millions who succeed and flourish in exactly the same world as those who recede and wither. We all become what we construct in our creative mind and poor friends will instil non creative thoughts into our minds, do not doubt this.

Face all reality, my Unknown Friend, learn to free yourself from worry, those who cannot, are in the shadow. If they could see what awaits them in the clear light of reality they would never worry again. Never worry if someone likes you or not. Become your own very best friend!

14. HEALTH ~ ILLNESS

You really do not know how long you are going to live for. Unknown Friend, value every single moment of your life, work in every way possible to keep yourself as fit and healthy as you can. Meditate when you can, and on one of your meditations, concentrate deeply and use the mantra.

"Body, keep healthy, guide me to eat the right food, allow me to sleep deeply, nurture me to partake in gentle exercise"

I am no doctor, I do not have to be, I know that if I have a clear mind, I know that if I eat the right foods, I know if I walk 4-5 miles each day, my body will be able to rest properly and I will be fit. You know this too, you know this as surely as the moon moves the sea, as surely as the planets orbit the sun.

You could attempt to try this for a week. Turn off the television, do not buy a newspaper, do not listen to the news, keep clear of negative people and situations, read some books, write a journal about yourself, your hopes and inspirations. Listen to as many varied pieces of music that you can, indulge yourself in culture and creativity.

Could you get up a little earlier and walk a mile or two? In the evening walk a little more, and whilst you walk, think about your hopes and inspirations, be realistic, think about being, healthy, happy, free from debt, free from mundane to Friday problems, think about being free. What is the humans greatest asset? It is time. What is our most valuable possession? It is the body. What should be our greatest objective? It must be Freedom. These positive actions and thoughts will help you to be healthy.

I ask you to *consider* trying each of these exercises. You may be surprised to find a powerful change occurs, the two exercises help you become disciplined in your day to day routine, they are like the monks long meditations, they teach you to connect your inner being.

We have choices to make in our lifetime. Most people procrastinate far too much. Most people do not look after their bodies. Most people do not look after their minds, they let the media and government guide them to what is right and wrong, they think the doctor will cure them from every illness. Truth to tell if you look after your mind and body you will never need to worry too much about you health.

I will introduce you to the bank balance of health, when we are born most of us are in good health. Imagine that you had a bank balance of health which was full, it had, let's say, 100 units of health in it. As you go through the early years of your life your bank balance of health continues to be full, as you grow older and eat the wrong foods, a little too much of what is nice, alcohol, sweet foods and less and less exercise, you take on many forms of debt, emotional stress begins to effect you, you do not realise it, but the bank balance of health is being spent, almost before you know it, the bank balance of health is in the red, soon you will be paying interest, the interest is called illness, you will have to start looking after yourself, if you exercise, eat the right foods, get plenty of rest, the debt can be repaid, and you go back into positive health! Meditate upon the bank balance of health, see if you can work out how many units of health you have already spent!

There are millions of words written about health. I do not worry about any of them. On the few occasions I have been ill, I have visited the doctor and taken the drug prescribed and I have returned to health, there are millions of people who have gone into hospital and come out cured and lived very long lives!

Be careful of what you read or whom you listen to, you may think I am cynical, maybe I am, however a lot of the books written about health and pseudo cures, are full of fact and figures and recycled fairy stories, I will bet a pound for a penny when the authors of these works of fiction become really ill, it will be a doctor, drugs and the services of a hospital which they will turn to, and will probably cure them. Assess for yourself what you think is right. The route to happiness and health is not rocket science. Good fresh food, exercise and rest are surely the principal keys to health.

Only yesterday (August 2012) Lizzy and I were talking to a young girl who was pregnant, as she smoked her cigarette, she told us that she had had a late night of drinking and was very tired and felt unwell. She said that she was looking forward to a few drinks after work "to cheer her up". You do not have to look very far before you hit on the real truth to health do you? Self neglect is the real place that problems begin.

Unknown Friend, you will free yourself from one less worry if you just do a little each day to benefit your health, each extra step you walk, each healthy meal you eat, each early bedtime, pays back the debts in the bank balance of health. There are illnesses which could await us, have a yearly check up with your doctor, keep yourself stress free and you will have very little to worry about your health.

15. SETBACK

Consider setbacks and failure as lifetime experiences which you can learn from, accept that they are the consequence of previous moments of poor choices and you will have learnt a valuable lesson.

You cannot see the Grand Canyon, unless you travel to it. You cannot own a car, unless you work for it. You cannot experience happiness, unless you seek it. You cannot experience unhappiness, unless you are within it. Every single experience you have, you are part of. The present state of mind you are in is due to your previous actions, decisions, choices, stagnation, motivation, thoughts, meetings, friends or even words you have read or listened to.

It is simply not possible to analyse the whole of your life and in truth why should you? Think about this very carefully, why should you attempt to work through your life to attempt to discover why you are where you are now? It makes not a jot of difference if you are in a good place or a bad place, or even who you are, you have made yourself who you are and that is the way it is.

All of the really successful people I have interviewed leave the past behind and focus upon being the very best they can be in anything they do. They do not consider set back or failure as a problem, they realise they cannot win every time.

Now, mark these words well, very little happens by chance. If you are constantly worrying and in difficulty, you are doing something wrong. The words in this book are written from observing very successful people and, I can write with certainty, 99% of them have taken years to become the person they are. You have to work, work, work, to find success. You have to work, work, work, to find constant happiness.

To go from a difficult situation to a good one may take weeks of effort, and you may have to realign yourself many times during the journey. A navigator sets to sea knowing his destination, if he encounters a storm along the way he will have to readjust his course, to get back in the right direction, in the same way, you may well have to readjust your thinking and beliefs many times during your life experience as well.

Constantly work to do everything properly with positive and intentional actions. For example, drive your car carefully, learn to speak clearly and properly, if you buy something, learn how to use it and learn all of it's functions, look after all of your possessions, take your time and be methodical in every thing that you do. Really care about the processes of life, it's the process that is important. Like it or not your mind is no more or no less than a memory bucket. If you become methodical in all of your actions, you will eventually realise everything can be learnt and that includes how to be worry free, and if you work to become free from worry, you will be happy, healthy and prosperous.

You must take action if you want something. You must act in the correct way to get whatever it is that you want. A really great friend of mine loves her holidays. Every year she saves like crazy and then goes to America and spends like crazy! I know this, if you went on a holiday to America with Kim you better hang onto your safety belt! Kim fills every moment of her day with exercise, then her job, then she looks after her incredible daughter. A few years ago she was in a time of shadows, she took her life back, no one is going to take it from her. Once she said to her partner "I love you, but I do not need these negative vibes around me, change or go" she really meant what she said, and out the door he went, the power of the action made him think, he came back a different man.

See every setback as over, past, finished and beneficial. Consistently work for your future, making certain that all of your present actions are positive, right, beneficial, moral, full of love, caring, purposeful, decisive. If you have a situation which needs deep thought then take the time to weigh up your choices. Many years ago I went through a time where my business was very poor, I had a lot of debts, I lost everything I possessed, even though my life was in turmoil on every level, I still knew that I was a very able and capable business man, as time has proven I was right, what I failed to accept at the time, was that I did not understand the processes of success, and, one of the most important lessons, which is, sometimes we have to cut our losses and start all over again. I have learnt from my failures and the dark cloud which used to be over me is now a silver lined existence!

You will find it more difficult to succeed if you have people around you who do not think you are able to succeed! A self limiting belief system is often developed from the words of others. If you have the slightest seed of doubt in your mind, you will need to deal with this promptly and efficiently. One of the most simplest solutions to overcome doubt is to write down what you want to achieve and how you are going to achieve it and do not worry about how long it will take to bring success to your project. Do not trust to holding a plan in the your head, your mind will change you will go off track, formulate your plan, and stick to it! The successful human does not worry about success or setback, he or she enjoys the journey of discovery.

Never worry about setbacks. Walk into your future and leave your past behind.

16. WORK

Using your time and energy to make others happy
depletes you and disempowers them. Using your time and
energy to find peace within and make yourself happy,
empowers you and inspires them. Nowhere is this more
true when it comes to work and the way in which you
earn your living. No matter what you do, no matter if you
like your work or not, put the very best effort into every
moment of it. We have all worked with the individual who
can never find satisfaction within the workplace, their
words become tiresome and can have the most depleting
effect upon all who work around them. Do not become
like these people, do not agree with these people, their
attitude can only do harm and cause discord. Whatever
you do, respect your work hours, save some money from
the fruits of your labour and never complain. If you are a
hard worker, you will never be without a job.

I have run my own business, driven trucks, worked in a
warehouse, worked in restaurants and bars and never

once have I thought the work below me. All have brought me in contact with good and bad people, great and pathetically selfish employers, and everything in between. My work life has been tough and sometimes extraordinary effort has been used for very little return, some of the work may not have been the best but you can be certain I put my very best into each and every job.

For the last eight years I have dedicated my life to my creativity, recording, film, photography, writing, I have known many lean days, however, I love my work, I put every effort into it, and now my efforts are really beginning to bear fruit. I have had many poor harvests and set backs, In this moment, I know my happiness, security and future are secure, this is as a direct result of putting the very most into everything I do.

Reward from work and effort is wonderful. The reward for the exchange of your life hours should be fair. Unfortunately, very often this is not the case, accept this, do not let this fact restrict you from ambition or working toward achieving greater reward. I accept these facts. I do not run from them. I know my life IS as valuable as any other, my blood would save the life of a King, a Queen, a child, a beggar, as would yours. We may not be born equal but I am certain we are all equal.

Is the effort of man equal? Of course it is, the man who drives a truck has exactly the same right to a decent wage as the man who sits in parliament or the senate. Why should life hours be worth any more or less because of the so called position of the job?

You must work for your security, work for your happiness, work for your freedom, never give a passing glance to what someone else has achieved or owns. In the final sleep, nothing matters, all that you accumulate will become someone else's. Work for today, and look after what you have earned, with not a care in the world for anyone else's material ideas.

Remember this phrase "success only comes before work in one place, the dictionary". It is a master key to success. Most of us are born at the bottom of the system and it requires effort and work to succeed in anything. Therefore, put your very best into everything that you do, you never know where or when a new opportunity will arise and those who are recognised as hard workers will always take the cherry! Those who complain or who are lazy receive the stone.

Should we accept our place in the social bee hive? We should if we are right minded, clear thinking and have the desire to happiness in our hearts, not just to make the best of our social standing, but to give ourselves a purpose and meaning to our existence, Again we can learn from nature, there are many animal and insect communities which have highly structured and organised systems. The beehive is a perfect example, each little bee works to fulfil it's purpose, thousands working together to the common good, the human race can learn so very much from nature's design.

Unknown Friend, I am not saying you should be subservient, controlled, or become a slave. I ask you to meditate upon the fact that we have to earn our wages through work and effort. This work and effort should give us a sense of wellbeing and if we live within our means, we will be without worry. As you build your inner strength you will overwhelm negative thoughts and attitudes, you will look after your possessions that you have worked for.

Access your attitude toward your work very carefully indeed, it takes up a lot of your life hours. You can meditate upon the choice between giving your very best or being indifferent. Do not enter your work place with a heavy heart, enter it with the attitude that you are there to pay for your home, food and wellbeing. I assure you, as you follow this path, the doors of opportunity will open as if by magic.

Unknown Friend never worry about having to work, be proud of the items you own, the food you eat which you have purchased due to your toil and effort! Work is part of the social system called civilisation.

17. AGE

The older you get the more life experience you have, do not doubt this truth. I put it to you that you have enough knowledge to achieve any goal. You may not have the wish or drive, but you do have the wisdom, understanding and knowledge available to you, should you desire to make any changes. This is an amazing truth, think about the words of truth "you cannot put a young head on old shoulders".

Unknown Friend, we have so many things in our lives which are still to be done, only fear and memories hold back the new opportunities and ambitions which await the explorer of life's golden years. You may be happy with your life as it is, you may be happy to allow your future to unfold from your past actions, thoughts, endeavours. Should you ever decide to take a new course or involve yourself in new plans, be certain that you are able to work from that moment of decision to enhance your health, truths and freedom, you have a whole life of encounters to draw upon. You cannot fail. You are the most important person in you life. As you accumulate the years of your lifetime your mind becomes full of beneficial tools which you can utilise. You do not even have to work very hard to allow them to rise to the conscious mind. Age is an asset not a restriction. Never think that life has passed you by, never think you are too old to start something new.

In the early stages of life, there is the power of youth, the thought that life will last forever, the stamina, youthful spirit and drive which literally drives desires to come into fruition, days somehow seem longer, and the lack of responsibilities such as mortgage, debt, looking too far ahead into the future and a badly maintained body are a long way away (or so it seems). The youthful are full of ideas and desires, they want to be famous, a desire which is so rarely achieved, they want to be really rich a desire that lingers far too long in far too many, some want to marry and have a family without the slightest regard to the commitment and responsibility involved, some travel the world, get a degree or do both, many do nothing but complain, many ruin their life right at the beginning, setting the seed of constant struggle until the desire to change for the better becomes their greatest desire.

This is the way it is! We could think about age in relation to the social system. There is no point to exploring this here, you can research the "system" for yourself. I am asking you to become free from worry through rational thought, no more no less. Wherever you are on your life journey, you can tune and finely adjust yourself and your situation to your benefit. You must accept without question that you are the most important person in your life. Yes, you can have deep bonding relationships and friendships, in fact these are fulfilling and beneficial to happiness. You will do well to accept that to be able to get the very best from any social interaction you need to be at your very best in every way. As you get older you learn how to behave in sociable ways, you learn patience, you are not restricted by age, age and experience are an advantage.

Age is no bar to success at any part of the process of life, one just has to learn to take advantage of where you are at any one moment. You are able to do this by honing your wisdom, knowledge and understanding to such a degree that difficult situations, or new opportunities, turn into advantages as if by magic. If you follow the truth and do not break the rules you will win 90% of the time and the other 10% will not matter!

Gale had a large house, her business earned a lot of money for her, she told me that she had decided to sell her home. " I am going to downsize, travel to the places I really wish to see, I have a desire to stay on a Pacific Island for a few months, travel through India, explore Australia and America. I am going to take a year out of my life as a reward for my hard work and effort. The sale of the house is causing problems with my children, they say that I am taking away my security, my answer to them is that I will still own a house it will just be a smaller one, they then told me that I should not be thinking about this "at my time in life" what they really mean Ian is that they think I am using their inheritance!" "that is a painful observation" I replied "No, it is a truthful one, in fact their belief that I was not able to make the right decisions or choices for myself really made me determined to make my plans a reality" Gale's age and wisdom had taken control, what a powerful lady she is.

Alex was about 24 when I met him, he told me "I have wasted *most* of my life I am not going to achieve anything now, what is there for me in life?" the answer to this was easy "You have very little at this moment in time, you have a lot of self limiting beliefs, you are not assessing your potentials, you have a lifetime ahead of you, you have too little faith in yourself, therefore you are in the best possible place you can be in to turn your life around and become a successful man" was my answer. "How do you know, you do not know me" he said with much anger in his voice. "Because you think your life is over before it has begun, therefore you know you have a problem, you are young, age and time is on your side" was my inevitable answer. I received an e-mail from Alex 3 years later, it read, "Hi Ian, You will not remember me, I was in a very low place when I spoke to you only 3 years ago, I am now working in Australia as a diving instructor and loving every moment of my life, I am now married to the girl of my dreams, we are saving for our own dive boat, my life is better than I could ever have imagined". How Alex achieved this extraordinary change in so short a time proves that one's age or present situation is no barrier to success.

I chose these two examples to guide you towards a fact, which is, older age and wisdom are a powerful combination, younger age and limiting belief can be potentially disastrous. At every moment during our lifetime we should be active, progressive and positive. These three words are very much part of securing a worry free life. There are many who are not mentored or guided to realising their full potentials. They have to find their own way, many capitulate, falsely feeling that life has not gone well for them or they have no time left. Or they are "at the wrong age". How wrong this assumption is.

Never worry about your age, the older you get, truly the wiser you are.

18. FREEDOM

"The amount of freedom you can access in your lifetime is the real gauge or indicator of your success" ~ Ian Timothy

Alain is a big man, with a big smile, he begins to laugh during the interview as he looks around "What's wrong with these people? They have access to food, a warm home, education, work, a reasonably safe society, they walk around with their chin on their chest and seem to complain about everything". I agree with him without question.

Alain comes from Cameroon. When you look at his face there is something not quite right, he has seen this questioning look before.

"They are not tribal scars you are looking at, they are machete wounds, I have them all over my body, the police did this to me when they discovered that I was warning the people who were on their hit list. I was lucky to have survived the beating, I had to flee for my life".

Alain became a refugee, finally settling in England, free but penniless. He worked until he had saved just over 200 pounds, he purchased a large cooking pot, a gas burner, paper plates, plastic forks, meat, spices, fruit and a few specialist vegetables, at his first outdoor market he got his investment back! The following week he attended 2 more markets, he purchased a small waterproof gazebo, he had a stainless steel fold up table made, and worked 7 days a week selling his fantastic Cameroonian food. People travel far and wide to eat the food he prepares at his permanent base in the city in which I live.

I comment "I suppose that you are very proud of your incredible success?"

"No, I am proud to live in and be part of a free society" he replies and he really means this, he really does.

Alain knows the real truth. Freedom is our most important objective. Freedom from pain, freedom from debt, freedom from slavery, freedom to act upon one's own desires, freedom to vote, freedom to say no, the list is endless.

One day each week I have a day walking alone, I take some photographs, I write one or two poems, I will think about my books, I have access to beautiful parks and incredible beaches. In fact there are very few people on the whole of this earth who could own a park or beach, and yet, I can freely find a beach, a park, a wood, a forest and walk and think to my hearts content! This is freedom.

I do not need a large house or many excessive possessions, as I value freedom from debt, far more than the slavery of social climbing or the damaging lie of greed. I value my life hours (the truth of time) far more than the illusion of wealth. I have more than enough for my needs. I never want for anything. It is almost as if constant happiness and good fortune comes into my life, due to my belief in freedom and my desire to be free from social, political, material, intellectual and emotional entrapment.

I do not trust to luck by the way, the more I reject luck, the luckier I become. I am convinced the more I think about, the more I talk about, the more I research, the more I demand freedom into my life, the wealthier I become.

Some individuals have an unachievable desire, they become imprisoned within it. For example, some people who have little money can become convinced they will win the lotto. There are people who want to become successful business entrepreneurs or want to be wealthy, without accepting hard work and effort is part of that difficult game. These are only two examples of day dreamers, living illusions. Luck, destiny and living pipe dreams usually imprison the weak and unwary.

This book is an example of the dedication needed, The project started ten months ago, it has been rewritten five or six times and before I release it, it will be proofread, ten copies will be hand printed for friends, they will send me feedback, when all is well the project will be finally printed and turned into an e-book! Unknown Friend, use the same single minded dedication in any thing that you do. Dedication has a reward called success, and success has a reward called freedom.

This book is part of my freedom. My CDs and my downloads are part of my freedom. I think of everything that I do as contributing to my freedom and everything becomes a labour of love. Unknown Friend, try this way of thinking, you will discover what the word 'magic' really means.

A few paragraphs ago I mentioned my creative day when I take photographs, write poems, walk and think. It is during this time that ideas come into my mind. I feel connected to, and resonate with, the incredible universe full of unfathomable secrets. I then reflect upon my insignificance when compared to the wonderment of creation. At this time I know what real freedom is, and I know, in being able to be free, these thoughts drive me to continue to work, to turn my potentials into realities.

Unknown Friend, find a creative day of deep meditation, when you do nothing but be alone and think! Find this peace, demand it as your right. During this time, you will find every part of your life becomes like pieces in a magical jigsaw puzzle and when you have completed this empowering exercise, you will discover, as each day passes, the picture of the purpose of life will become clearer. I already know what the picture will be. It is you, Unknown Friend, it is YOU.

Find this creative day, if you cannot find a day in a week, find a day in a month. If you cannot find a day in a month, find a day in a year. Do not dare to think that you have not got the time to do so, because in a very short time indeed you will enter the final sleep. When you are brave enough to be at one with yourself, (ask yourself now, when did you take yourself away from your home, family and friends, to be intentionally on your own?) you will experience real freedom, the chains of the mundane are broken forever, and the paradoxical realisation of your insignificance in the universe and the fact you are the most important person in it, drives you to live every moment to the full and find more of the most beautiful experience of all, which is called freedom.

There are men and women who work to free the world from oppression. Seek them out and be inspired by them, support them in your mind. There will be those who work to bring the world to be at peace. Seek them out and support them in your mind. There are those who work to feed the world, seek them out and support them in your mind. Their work, which is to free mankind from anything which impinges upon it's freedom, is so very important, for their example guides the whole human race to work together to find the bliss of freedom, only when the power of freedom is available to all, will we be sure that we can continue to exist upon this planet of beauty.

Believe in the power of freedom and you assist your mind to be a little closer to being free of worry.

19. REGRET

At a conference, I was talking to a very large group of delegates and in the audience a man took exception to my talk! Nothing new, I do not often 'go with the flow'!

After the conference, he came over to speak to me, and he proceeded to tell me why I was so very wrong. On every point he made, I agreed with him and slowly his anger began to subside, his frustration diminished, his words became kinder.

Finally I asked "do you feel it is better to listen to the whole story? Or consider one part of the story is the whole story"? His answer was "it is better to listen to the whole story". I then said "I have listened to your whole story, without question or comment, you have given me food for thought, I have *no regrets* about anything I have said today, I hope that you will forgive me for upsetting you, I put forward points of view which can be accepted or not, in the same way you have just put forward your points of view which I can accept or not."

I had *no regrets* with agreeing to disagree, the man's intentions were of the highest order, even though his words did not resonate with my reasoning, he had a right to his thoughts, and I accepted this. He wanted to change my mind and enforce his beliefs upon me, he did not succeed.

A mind becomes frustrated if another mind does not agree with it. Frustration is the fuel of anger, to accept that others have a right to their opinion, leaves you free from regretting something you may do or say whilst you are trying to defend your point of view.

To agree with someone in this way is not an easy way out of confrontation, it is, in fact, a very valuable life skill.

Unknown Friend, each of us encounter the emotion of regret, Wiki says, regret is a negative conscious and emotional reaction to personal past acts. Regret is distinct from guilt which is a deeply emotional form of regret. On one hand there is regret for certain actions, on the other, there is regret for inaction.

The latter is more important to consider, that is, regret formed from inaction, You are only here once and I invite you to live your life to the full To my mind we must strive to enjoy every moment. From this standpoint, I ask you to free yourself from the regrets of the past (as I have pointed out to you the past is set in stone and cannot be changed) and live a full and meaningful life, in which you enjoy every moment, experience everything you can, and work towards attaining the wonderful pleasures life has to offer. There is very little we cannot do if we put our minds to it.

My work is so fulfilling, I talk to people and record their thoughts, I then formulate my recordings from what I have listened to. The two words I hear very often are "I wish". Every time they come into the conversation there will be the excuses, I had my children too early, I dropped out of Uni, I did not do what I wanted to do, my parents were...etc and I know these "I wish" statements are stories of regret.

What do you wish for? What do you actually want? Consider this, if you are working to an objective, your mind will become focussed upon that objective, nothing else can affect you. Viktor Frankl guided us with these words "Give a man an objective and he will go to any lengths to achieve that objective!" who are we to argue with Viktor? He asks you not to think about doing the things that make you happy, He asks you not to make positive decisions that free you of regrets, He asks you not to formulate objectives that will bring freedom into your being. He asks you not to think of a blue tree, and now, you are thinking of a blue tree!

I have a friend called Wendy, she is a very special person. She had experienced a betrayal by two friends and she had been really hurt. The two men had committed a serious crime and were sentenced to very hefty terms in prison. Unfortunately for Wendy two things had occurred, one was that she was known by association to them and secondly she had lent them a lot of money. She was at her wits end "what should I do?" she asked "Wendy if there was anything in the world you could do what would it be?" was my reply "Africa, I would like to go to Africa" she said. "Then get a job, work every hour that you are given, pay your debts, and save to go to Africa." Two years later she went on her first visit to Africa, she is already planning her second trip. "Do you have any regrets?" I asked her recently. "No, I have a life to live and a world to see, I haven't got time for regrets."

Why worry about anything? There is no point whatever is there? (There can be only one answer to this question.) The moment we have an obstacle in our path which causes concern, do something about it, pay off the debt, say goodbye to the fool, move from the house, change the job, just do not have any regrets for not making the change or taking forward moving, positive action. Most of all, always do the things that you want to do, in the way you know is right for you. I ask you to regret nothing you have done, I ask you to turn all negative emotion into a positive and powerful asset by saying to oneself "every experience, no matter what the outcome, was in fact a beneficial lesson".

I write of the 'Path of Truths', the path is your life, the truths are the experiences of your life, you must accept all of them. On the pathway you will encounter regrets, setbacks, moments of joy, love, happiness and many more 'moments'. Regret not one of them, each and every one has made you who you are. Each of them can drive you to who you want to be.

Meditate upon this mantra, "I will never have any regrets because of inaction".

20. MONEY

Consider money as a unit of exchange for life hours. Each hour of your lifetime is exchanged for tokens which you can then exchange for anything that you need, want or desire. No more or no less, whatever you save is the excess you accumulate after your requirements have been purchased. There is no other way of looking at money.

There are many people who have a desire to own more than they can afford. They borrow money to rent the item they want, yes rent the item, it is not theirs until the final payment is made. Those who lend the money work with pieces of paper which apparently represent the money which is borrowed. No money changes hands. The banker just says, "I have the money in my reserves, I will guarantee your payment and I will charge you interest for my loan" lets clarify this. A builder borrows money to buy some land, he borrows some money to buy the materials to build a house, the bank guarantees the loans and puts numbers on the account of the people who sell the land

and the materials to the builder. The banker has not actually used any money at all he has only made a promise that the money is available to be used to buy the land and the materials. The numbers he has put upon the accounts of the sellers of the land and building materials, can be used by them to buy the items they need. A man sees the house the builder has built and wishes to buy it, he has saved a deposit, which he gives to the banker, who then adds some numbers to the builder's account, The man moves into the bank's house and pays his rent, the house is not his until he has made the final payment, during this transaction the man may see another house. The bank allows him to sell their house and keep some of the profit which it takes back as a larger deposit for the new and bigger house.

At some time during his life time the man finally owns the house. He purchased it 25 years ago for 100000 tokens and it is now worth 250000 tokens. In fact, when you take inflation into account, the house is in real terms, worth the same price as when it was purchased. Truth to tell when interest and maintenance is taken into account the man has made nothing! What happens now? He can sell his house and realise the asset or live without rent until he dies. The only real winner is the banker who has converted the man's life hours into many more numbers on his balance sheet. The final outcome is interesting because when the man dies all that he has worked for becomes someone else's, at the moment of death all that you own has gone.

The banker has learnt how to make you a slave. It will punish you if you break his rules or try to escape.

I was talking to an Italian, he told me in the 50's and 60's Italy was considered a poor country, even though you could walk through the streets of Milan and Turin and see many people enjoying life, there were Vespa and Lambretta scooters everywhere, Fiat 500 cars in abundance, "no one paid any tax, we all bartered and lived on the black market, there was a real community, hustle and sharp practice yes, but times were good, there was no state help, we got on with life". Is this rose coloured glasses the man looked through when he told me his story? To some degree I am sure, but there is some real truth in the observation. As the government of world has become more astute at extracting tax from the population, the bartering, the children working for cash at the weekend, the mother washing for a few extra tokens is becoming a system of the past. The strange observation is there is now more poverty, more struggle, more unhappiness. The Governments over tax the population and squander the loot. They also brainwash the weak minded into thinking it is a crime to try at any cost to make ends meet, by saying it is shameful not to declare everything one earns. There is no argument that if one takes a state benefit that one then has to abide by the rules. But for those who are struggling to make ends meet surely the end justifies the method, why should a gardener not be able to sell his surplus, a beekeeper not be able to sell his honey, a pensioner not be able to charge for a dress repair, a young man not take a few tokens in exchange for cleaning a car or mowing a lawn?

The governments have learnt how to make you a slave. It will punish you if you try to escape. This effects your right to freedom.

That is the meditation, the token called money has its source in your life hours. Who wants to take your life hours? Those who own land which has resources, oil, coal, iron, minerals, they are at the top of the industrial tree. Those who manipulate the tokens are called bankers, they are at the top of the money tree. The illusionists who smoke screen your real existence, they are at the top of the entertainment tree. Those who manipulate your life are called politicians, they are at the top of the incompetent tree. All of these and many more have learnt how to funnel your life hours into their pockets.

Just so you know, there is no need to worry about the system. It is out of control, sooner or later we all come to realise the benefit of culturing a sensible material attitude, I cannot guide you, there is nothing more to write on this subject, you either live within your means and have no worries, or you live beyond your means and invite a source of so many worries into your life.

21. HAPPINESS

Happiness is a right, not a reward, Happiness is a way of life, not a moment in time to be remembered ~ Ian Timothy.

There are many really great books about finding happiness and you will learn a new gem of wisdom in each of them, buy them all! You will now have realised, my point of view is that one must educate the mind and one must constantly and consistently work for success in everything we do. Happiness is no exception.

I have a big top loading washing machine, it has 4 wash programmes and it is simple in it's design. It is the second one I have owned. The first one stopped working when it's gear box failed, nothing too interesting you may think, apart from the fact that when I looked at the serial numbers on the whirlpool site, I discovered it was made in 1973 it was just short of 40 years old, I had owned it for ten years and it never once let me down, the new one is exactly the same design and in a strange way, it makes me happy. I like its simplicity, I like its heavy build, I love the way it works. I trust it to do its job. In fact, it is far more reliable than many people I have known in my life and I include my self in the team of unreliable people!

I have to confess the first washing machine would still be working if I had not broken it! My brother was moving house and he brought 3 weeks of laundry for me to wash, I overloaded the machine and damaged the gear box. The machine may only be metal, however I was unhappy about the fact that I contributed to its demise. It proves you can have a liking for many things! And I learnt a valuable lesson.

Happiness is just like the washing machine. When you find the right partner, find the right situation, find the right job, find the right way of life they will work for and with you, so long as you do not abuse or overload them.

Very often the simple pleasures will bring the greatest happiness. If we look and think carefully we will find we are already in a place of happiness. We might see something or see someones lifestyle and think the object or the other person's way of life may bring more happiness than we already have and we falsely lead ourselves to believe there is another better happiness somewhere else.

Earlier in the week I was in the city and I looked into a jeweller's window. In the window there was a watch which had a price tag of 23000 pounds. Whist sitting in the bus on my journey home I began to think about the watch. The question I asked myself was this, "Would the person who purchased the watch actually feel a greater degree of happiness from owning the watch, than the overwhelming happiness I feel when I look at my sunflowers?"

This is a big question, because he might have purchased the watch for many reasons, he could have brought it as a present, perhaps the act of giving such an expensive gift would have made him and the receiver of the gift very happy indeed, I do not know for certain, I feel that happiness is constant, whether it is sunflowers or a Rolex whatever makes you happy, is working for you, so do not try to change it.

Therefore, is it the emotion which we should search for? Or is the emotion already there and it just needs activating? Is the search for happiness a futile quest? I think it is, I think happiness is like a pool of water that dries up, unless it is constantly refilled with goodness, right thinking, appreciation for the small gifts we are given and kind words between family and friends. Emotions cannot be purchased. There is no shop on earth where you can buy love, happiness, mental health or wellbeing and there never will be.

You may feel that the next comment is going to be something like the constantly recycled statement that possession is only short term happiness. In fact I am going to say to you that possessions can, and will, bring you happiness and you should never feel any guilt for owning anything. If you have worked for what you want and you are not entering a long term debt or you have incorrectly assessed your priorities then do it, buy it, love it!

The bike I am saving for, the washing machine I use, the camera, the expensive microphone, my Mac computer, my clothes, the good quality food I buy, all contribute toward my pool of emotions being full of happiness. Realism has a part to play, it's no use me thinking that the 23000 pound watch would or could bring me happiness, because, for one point I could not afford it and for a second point I do not wear a watch (and never will).

Only when you covert something you cannot afford, will you drain the pool of emotion called happiness. You can be sure Unknown Friend, if I won the lotto, my first purchase would be a bottle of Dom Perignon, my second would be a Porsche (well I am human). And if I do not? I already have my wonderful partner, I will have my bike, my own happiness, my incredible friends and my washing machine! I cannot lose.

There are 22 questions I ask the people whom I interview, each of the questions are the names of each chapter of this book. So let me finish this short chapter with the answer I received from two of the questions I asked a man called Jason.

Jason is a 39 year old business man, I really liked him, his openness and bright personality must be a factor in his success.

"Jason, What brings happiness into your life?"

"I have more than my fair share of happiness, a really successful business, a very happy family life, I love my wife and two children, we all work together and everyone knows I do not work at weekends. Saturday and Sunday are my reward for my week's work, I will answer e-mails, I will not answer business calls. When I started out, I worked seven days a week and up to eighteen hours each day, I had no time for anything other than my work, I met and married my wife when I was 30 and that is when my happiness really started"

"Jason, Does money contribute to happiness?"

"Without a doubt my answer is yes, Kelly and I do not have to worry about bills, we have a beautiful house, two fantastic holidays every year, sun and sand late June, a cruise late September, then there is a week of Christmas happiness, without the success of the business these wonderful moments could never happen"

"Could you live without the wealth you have accumulated?"

"I do not consider the question relevant"

Read how Jason answered the third question. That's the way of successful people, if there is not a problem there, they will not attempt to find an answer to it. Of more interest is the answer to the first question, Jason's happiness is his family and his ability to separate work from his greatest happiness. He really is a great man. I really enjoyed our time together. Jason inspired me.

Happiness is a pool of emotion which needs to be constantly filled, you can fill it with good thoughts, kindness, generosity, love, family and friends, music, books, looking after your body, looking after your possessions, or any of the million and one gifts of goodness that are available to us. I guide you to be constantly doing that which is right, and focusing upon bringing happiness to yourself and those who are in your Universe.

By contributing to the pool of happiness, you will be one step closer to becoming free from worry.

22. SILENCE

Unknown Friend, it is very early in the morning, the city I live in is nearly silent, and I think of you. Every word in this book has been written with you at my side. I do not know you, in the same way as I will never know Brenda Ueland, who was the woman who taught me how to write, I will never know Valentin Tomberg, who taught me the most incredible spiritual lessons, I will never know Pamela Colman Smith, who drew the images which have provoked me to enter into deep and meaningful meditations and yet these Unknown Friends are as influential as any human I have ever actually met.

If you research (which means to look again) you will discover that the experts tell us we crave friendships and relationships. Does this mean that because we are told this is, this is *actually* what we need? I find this difficult to believe. When I sit on the bus which takes me into the city, people seem to want to be in their own space, they seem to like to be in their oneness. I actually think that a bus is one of the best meditational areas we can ever enter! When the selfish teenager plays his loud music, the other passengers resent his encroachment upon their moment of peace. I think we do need to find solitude from time to time, we do not have to be surrounded with family and friends every moment of our existence. If you learn to love yourself, you will never be lonely.

I cannot hear my mind working and you cannot have listened to the mind of anyone who has spoken to you. You have listened to their words, but are their words their thoughts? Are the words you speak really the thoughts you hold as your truth? My goodness, you will have to think carefully about this question.

Unknown Friend, you are reading my words, the pages of this book cannot speak, my words on the page are silent and they speak to you! The blade of grass grows, you cannot hear its growth, the tree grows, you cannot hear its growth, your blood flows, your lungs take oxygen into the blood, the oxygen is used by every cell in your body and all is silent except for the beat of the heart and the whispering sound of your breathing.

Your thoughts are silent. You do not know how you instantly remember the words to a song you have not listened to for 20 years, and yet the memory of the words are there. All of the knowledge you have learnt is within your mind ready to be used in an instant. This is an amazing proof of the wonder and complexity of your mind and body.

The silent library called memory can provide you with the information which can be used to your advantage or it can destroy your lifetime! And just like the old record which opens the book of words to the song, the librarian of the mind will open any of the books of knowledge you choose to study. The librarian of the mind does not censor your desires, if you ask for a memory it will silently provide the fiction or fact you ask for.

In silent meditation you can rearrange your thoughts, you can concentrate carefully to train the librarian of the mind to guide you to use only the most useful memories. Simply explained you meditate (just for a minute or two a day) upon the positive, realistic and useful thoughts and ideas which are beneficial to you in your lifetime. The more you do this, the calmer you will become, and possibly you will think before you speak or learn the ability to stay silent.

Find a few minutes each day and meditate to find inner peace and silence. You will eventually find it, do not worry if it takes days or weeks, just take two or three minutes, as you wake up or just as you drift off to sleep and say to yourself 'bring a state of silence and peace into my mind'. Then, there will be a moment when you think about the power of these words, and your inner mind will take comfort from your conscious effort, to allow peace and silence into *your* 'being'.

There is an ultimate objective in life called freedom. You do not need any material possessions to take you to this sublime place. When you sleep you rest your body and your mind goes into the place of dreams and repair, nightmares are the way we dispose of our fears, dreams are where we experience the incredible potentials of our creativity. Successful fictional authors are only using dream like imagination when they write their books, and, very often, they write their very best work when they are alone and in silence.

I encourage you to seek the silence which will free you from worry. How can silence free you from worry? It will, because it does! In silence we can decide to pay off the debt, accept you are not a business entrepreneur, accept you are not going to be a millionaire, accept you will have to work for a living, accept you are a mighty fine person, accept you are at the centre of your universe, accept the person you are and how you look. Once you accept the truth of your situation, you then change your attitude, adjust your beliefs, make peace with your demons, and get back onto the 'right' path.

Like it or not, there is a right path to peace, love and harmony. There is also the wrong path which will take you into the unknown. Paradoxically, the right path is often one of silence and simplicity. The wrong path is full of gossip, bar room fiction, idealistic illusion, television soap shows, politician's lies, credit card debt, a house full of useless objects, holidays to nowhere, lottery pipe dreams and many more illusions! All of which lead the unwary pilgrim to think that they are walking toward the destination of fulfilment.

I am not saying for a moment that you cannot follow the path of material happiness, I only ask you to be realistic in your approach to life. If you want to be free from worry, be clear in your mind, you will always have to pay the piper. Only a silent clear thinking mind will realise, sometimes the piper's price, is too high a price to pay.

23. DEATH

Ask yourself if, when you die, will the memories of the way you lived your lifetime continue to exist in the memories of others? If you follow a truthful life journey, then the memories your friends, relatives and family have of you, will have a very good chance of continuing for many moons to come. Surely this is the past life existence that one should constantly work to achieve? Let me be clear, I feel that it is the memory of one's actions in life that can be the only realistic hope of life after death

The last nine years of my life have been a constant pleasure, and if I had only lived for those last nine years I would have had a 'life well lived'. I write of this again, because it indicates to you, that no matter where you are, or have been, on your life journey, you only need a few years of happiness to compensate for many years of difficulty. Never give up on yourself! I do not regret my past and nor should you! There are many years ahead of us. The years of the past can be useful, but the years ahead are the ones that really matter.

I am certain every moment counts. Unknown Friend, never waste a second in negative thought (what you 'think' you become). Your actions determine your future. Think, act, live, as if each moment is your last. The certainty of the final sleep should drive you to live your lifetime to it's greatest potential.

We all *should* seek a real oneness with human kind, we *should* culture a positive and progressive attitude towards the evolution of the world and everything in it, we *should* work together to achieve this, these are the social commitments and responsibilities all humans *should* learn. You may never be remembered for attempting to fulfil these moral obligations to the social beehive, this does not matter, just trying is enough. Live in a positive way and enjoy your lifetime, and you will be remembered for what you have achieved. What more could you ask for?

There are thousands who visit the medium in an attempt to communicate to a long lost family member or a friend, they grasp any tenuous link, any hope, attempting to make anything fit. One word, one confirmation, that's all they want, that's all they need to give them the proof that life exists after death. Millions of words written and spoken about the subject and not one jot of actual evidence of existence after death.

And what about these 'mediums'? They speak of life after death and reincarnation? Let them prove by their words. Let them speak to you with accuracy about your relatives who are on "the other side", let them prove that you can waste this lifetime because the next lifetime will be better, let them prove that you made a choice to be here, and if they cannot, then live this lifetime at the centre of your universe. Lifetime is for the living, leave the dead well alone, only in the everlasting sleep you will find the truth.

During the final sleep, the vessel which was our body decomposes, the atoms are liberated to become something else, nothing is wasted, a tree may grow over you, it will use the minerals that are released from your decomposition, and soon, someone will be breathing the oxygen the tree produces. Now that is magic, nothing really disappears, all is recycled. Do not have any fear of the final sleep, you only close your eyes, for one last time. There should be no reflection upon the final moment, never worry about the inevitable, it is a pointless task.

Your mind and thoughts are your own, *now* is the moment, what is behind you has gone, what is in front of you has not yet happened. If you imagine a long railway track which represents time, then imagine that you are represented by a carriage rolling along the track for the period of your lifetime, the actual length of your life does not matter, because you only exist in the carriage as it rolls along the track of time!

Never worry about the when, the how, the where, of the final sleep. You are travelling in this moment of life, on the track of existence, behind you the journey of the past, in front of you the unknown destination. Be certain you will close your eyes to the final sleep. And before you do Unknown Friend, learn to worry about nothing and live every second of your life to the full.

These are the final moments within this meeting place, which is this book. You may well find it will have a subtle effect on your 'being'. As I was writing it, I can say for certain, it has influenced the way that I look at my life. The twenty-two chapters are all truths which blend into one truth. I can say that I have really enjoyed our time together. So until we meet again, I wish you well and I know that, very soon, you will learn to 'Never Let Anything Worry You'

Ian Timothy
September 2012

28260757R00065

Made in the USA
Charleston, SC
06 April 2014